JOE MONTANA

THE ACHIEVERS

JOE MONTANA

Comeback Quarterback

Thomas R. Raber

Lerner Publications Company ■ Minneapolis

This edition of this book is available in two bindings:
Library binding by Lerner Publications Company
Soft cover by First Avenue Editions
241 First Avenue North
Minneapolis, Minnesota 55401

LIBRARY OF CONGRESS CATALOGING-IN-PUBLICATION DATA

Raber, Tom.
  Joe Montana, comeback quarterback/Tom Raber.
  p.   cm.   —(The Achievers)
  Summary: A biography with emphasis on the football career
of Joe Montana from his college days to his Super Bowl
victories.
  ISBN 0-8225-0486-3 (lib. bdg.)
  ISBN 0-8225-9572-9 (pbk.)
  1. Montana, Joe, 1956-   —Juvenile literature. 2. Football
players—United States—Biography—Juvenile literature. [1.
Montana, Joe, 1956-   . 2. Football players.] I. Title. II. Series.
GV939.M59R33   1989
796.332′092—dc20
[B]
                                                89-34353
                                                CIP
                                                AC

Manufactured in the United States of America

International Standard Book Number: 0-8225-0486-3 (lib. bdg.)
International Standard Book Number: 0-8225-9572-9 (pbk.)
Library of Congress Catalog Card Number: 89-34353

4   5   6   7   8   9   10   99   98   97   96   95   94   93   92   91

Contents

1

92 Yards to Go

Just 3 minutes, 10 seconds remained in the NFL season. The Cincinnati Bengals were leading the San Francisco 49ers, 16-13, and seemed almost certain of being crowned champions of Super Bowl XXIII.

More than 75,000 fans at Joe Robbie Stadium in Miami had just seen the Bengals kick a 40-yard field goal. The kick gave the American Football Conference champions a three-point lead and a blast of enthusiasm. It seemed that January 22, 1989, would be the Bengals' day.

The 49ers had possession of the football. But because of a holding penalty on the kickoff return, they were stuck on their own 8-yard line. They were 92 long yards away from a touchdown, and 65 to 70 yards away from being within range for a tying field goal. It was likely to be San Francisco's last chance with the football.

On the Bengals' sideline, some Cincinnati players were ready to celebrate. "We got 'em now," Cincinnati's Cris Collinsworth heard a teammate say. But Collinsworth, the Bengals' veteran wide receiver, knew it was too early to relax. "Have you taken a look at who's quarterbacking the San Francisco 49ers?" he asked his teammate. As long as Joe Montana was at quarterback for the 49ers, many people believed San Francisco had a good chance to come back. Montana had a reputation for bringing his teams from behind to win. Since his college days at the University of Notre Dame, and through 11 seasons with the 49ers, Joe had played his best when big games were on the line.

Now, everyone in the stadium and millions of fans watching television waited to see if Joe Montana could deliver one more time.

"Let's go, be tough," Joe told the 49ers in the huddle. Joe then hit running back Roger Craig with a pass for an 8-yard gain. He found tight end John Frank with another pass, this one good for 7 yards. Then Joe passed to wide receiver Jerry Rice for another 7 yards.

The 49ers were moving. But time was short. No Super Bowl had ever been decided by a touchdown this late in the game. When the pressure is on, many quarterbacks try to think of everything—and they can't think at all. Even Joe admitted later he was getting pretty nervous during this Super Bowl drive. But he kept his cool.

He handed off twice to Roger Craig who ran for short gains. Then Joe hit Jerry Rice and Craig with a series of passes, and suddenly the 49ers were on the Bengals' 10-yard line.

The noise in the stadium was deafening. Joe had marched San Francisco 82 yards in 10 plays. He had completed seven of eight passes. There were 34 seconds left, and now the 49ers had a chance to win.

Joe had been shouting to his teammates at the top of his voice through the entire drive. He was dizzy and exhausted. Up in the stands, Joe's mother Theresa was thinking back to the 1979 Cotton Bowl when Joe led Notre Dame in an amazing comeback victory over Houston. It looked like her son might do it again.

Many 49ers fans were reminded of the 1981 National Football Conference title game, when Joe's touchdown pass in the last minute had capped a remarkable drive that defeated the Dallas Cowboys.

Joe's wife Jennifer was also pulling for him. In his equipment bag that day, Jennifer had packed a T-shirt recalling the 49ers' Super Bowl victory over the Miami Dolphins in 1985. Joe wore it under his uniform jersey for good luck against the Bengals.

"Twenty halfback, curl, X-up," Joe called in the huddle. The play was to be a pass to Roger Craig, who would be swinging out of the backfield. But as the 49ers broke out of the huddle, something was wrong. Running back Tom Rathman had lined up on the left side of Montana, exactly where Roger Craig was supposed to be.

There was no time to argue, so Craig took the spot where Rathman should have been and the play went on. Joe looked first for Craig. But Roger was being double-teamed by the Bengals and couldn't break open.

Joe then looked to the other side of the field for his second choice—wide receiver John Taylor. Joe threw a pass to Taylor deep in the end zone. Taylor caught it and slammed it to the ground in celebration.

Joe's pass to wide receiver John Taylor capped San Francisco's last-minute touchdown drive and made the 49ers Super Bowl champions for the third time.

The 49ers had done it. With the extra point kick, they took a 20-16 lead and held it until the clock ran out. They had been Super Bowl champions in 1982 and 1985, and now they had won it in 1989. Each time, Joe Montana had been their quarterback.

Jerry Rice, who had played with a sprained ankle, was named the game's Most Valuable Player. He made 11 catches, many of them spectacular, and set a Super Bowl record of 215 yards receiving.

But much of the talk after the game was of Joe Montana. Once again he had come through in the clutch. He completed 23 of 26 passes for 357 yards, breaking the Super Bowl record of 340 yards set a year earlier by Washington's Doug Williams. In the second half—when it was most needed—Joe passed for 214 yards and two touchdowns.

"He's the greatest big-game player I've seen, period," said 49er offensive lineman Randy Cross. Boomer Esiason, the Bengals' talented quarterback said, "You saw the reason today that when Montana's career is over, he'll be remembered as a legend." And Cris Collinsworth, the opponent who wouldn't count Joe out, called Montana the greatest to play the game. "Joe Montana is not human," Collinsworth said. "I'm sure he did it in peewee football, in high school and college, and now in professional football. Every time he has had the chips down and people counting him out, he has come back."

2

Passing Tests

Joe Montana takes the snap and prepares to pass. He has about three seconds to decide where to throw. All around him is a blur of uniforms—the defense rushing in and his blockers working to protect him.

There's no time to recognize each player by face and number. Joe must have a feeling about when defenders are chasing him from behind and where his receivers are likely to break free.

Joe calls this "feeling color." When he senses less red, white, and gold of the 49ers around him—and more of the colors of the opposition—he can "feel" the color changing. He knows he must react.

Joe is well respected for thinking quickly under pressure. He's also known for having the moves to escape trouble and make something of a play that seems to be going nowhere. He is especially gifted at throwing while off balance or on the run.

These talents are hard to learn. Much of Joe's ability comes to him naturally. But since he was a boy, Joe has worked to develop his natural ability. Very early, he nurtured the mental outlook that would make him a top competitor.

Joe's first pass receiver was his father. Joe would often sit on the front steps at home, waiting for Joe Sr. to return from his job at a finance company. Joe Sr. would be tired sometimes, but he'd always make time to play with his son.

The Montanas would work out in a neighbor's yard where there was a tire swing. Mr. Montana would swing the tire. This would give Joe a moving target for his passes. Joe's dad also ran pass patterns. When they were through, the Montanas would play catch and talk over what they'd worked on.

Joe had no brothers or sisters to join in the practice. But sometimes a neighbor boy would play. The neighbor would pretend to be Jim Seymour, a star receiver for Notre Dame in the 1960s, and Joe would pretend to be Terry Hanratty, Notre Dame's outstanding quarterback. Even then, Joe dreamed of playing at the University of Notre Dame, a school with a history of winning football teams.

Joe Montana was born June 11, 1956, and grew up in Monongahela, Pennsylvania, about 30 miles from Pittsburgh. "Mon City," as the local people call it, is an area of mines, mills, farms—and enthusiasm for football.

Western Pennsylvania has been home to star quarterbacks Joe
Namath (above), Johnny Unitas, George Blanda, Dan Marino,
and Joe Montana.

At least four other outstanding professional quarterbacks also have come from western Pennsylvania: Johnny Unitas, Joe Namath, George Blanda, and Dan Marino.

But Joe didn't have many professional sports heroes while he was growing up. He was more wrapped up in his own play. He never went to Pittsburgh to see a Steelers or a Pirates game. In fact, the first time Joe saw the Steelers play in person, he was playing against them for the 49ers.

Joe was eight years old when he first played organized football. He also played Little League baseball and soon he was playing organized sports all year around.

By age 10, Joe felt burned out on sports. He saw kids having fun at other activities and he was envious. He wanted to quit football and join the Cub Scouts.

Joe's father wanted his son to be happy. But he was concerned when Joe said he wanted to quit. The football team had been practicing a few weeks already, and Joe would be letting his teammates down. Mr. Montana didn't want his son to walk away from something he had already started. He said that Joe must finish the season and then make up his mind about dropping football.

Joe finished the season, and he changed his mind about quitting. He also learned a lesson about being dedicated to his teammates and his goals. Today Joe credits his parents for building his competitive spirit. The Montanas believed that the desire to win was a healthy goal and worth Joe's effort.

As a teenager, Joe was all-America in football, all-state in basketball, and a star in baseball for the Ringgold High School Rams. At the time, basketball was Joe's favorite sport. He loved the constant action. He thought of it as being like a game of tag because it demanded lots of moving and darting. Joe found these skills helpful in escaping tacklers in football. Joe was also a great jumper, and although he was only 6 feet, 2 inches tall, he could make creative dunk shots and clear 6 feet, 9 inches in the high jump.

North Carolina State, a college with a rich basketball tradition, offered Joe a basketball scholarship. But Joe figured he was not quite tall enough for pro basketball. The college level would be as far as he could go with the sport.

Instead, football was going to be his game. By his junior year in high school, Joe was getting letters from dozens of highly regarded colleges known for their strong football programs. But from the beginning, Joe had his heart set on Notre Dame. He hoped that playing for the Fighting Irish would be a springboard for his lifelong goal—to be a professional football player.

Notre Dame was also Joe's father's favorite school. The Montanas believed that their son had the ability to be a professional athlete. But they also knew the importance of a good education. The Montanas hoped that a degree from Notre Dame would give their son opportunities that they had never had.

Joe found life difficult at Notre Dame. School was demanding. There were no easy courses, and the professors didn't favor anyone just because he was a football player. Joe was a conscientious student, but he was overwhelmed by the academic pressure.

Joe was also lonely. Before he went to Notre Dame, Joe had never been away from home alone. He had always taken vacations with his parents, often enjoying quiet fishing trips in Canada. At school, Joe missed his family and he called home often.

Even worse, Notre Dame had recruited six other freshman quarterbacks in 1974. Joe's first job with the team was to imitate the upcoming opponent's quarterback during practice. He didn't even learn any Notre Dame plays during the first year. Even in games just for freshmen, Joe played little.

By his sophomore year, 1975, Joe's grades were suffering. He knew making the pros was a long shot, so he bore down on his studies to prepare for a career outside of football. Both in the classroom and in football, Joe wanted to improve.

Joe got his first chance to play in the third game of the 1975 season. First-string quarterback Rick Slager was injured in the first quarter against Northwestern.

Joe at Notre Dame

Notre Dame was driving toward the Wildcats' goal. Joe came in and took the Fighting Irish in to score and then led them to a 31-7 victory.

Two weeks later, Joe entered a game against North Carolina in the fourth quarter. Notre Dame was losing, 14-6, but Joe gave the team a lift. Late in the game, Notre Dame was set to try a running play. But Joe changed the play at the line of scrimmage by calling a different signal. He threw a quick pass to Ted Burgmeier, who ran for an 80-yard touchdown. The play won the game for Notre Dame. It also won respect for Joe Montana, who had made a bold move by changing signals at the line of scrimmage.

The next season, Joe seemed poised to be Notre Dame's number-one quarterback. But he suffered a separated shoulder in pre-season practice and was out for the year. That 1976 season was frustrating, and Joe called it one of the worst years of his life. But Notre Dame "redshirted" Joe for the season. That meant that Joe would be held out of all games that season, even if he was well enough to play. It also meant that the season would not count against his eligibility. Joe could play an extra season to make up for the one he had missed.

The 1977 season marked Joe's third year of eligibility. But Joe felt almost as frustrated as he had been as a freshman. He was Notre Dame's third-string quarterback behind Rusty Lisch and Gary Forystek.

In the third game of the season, Notre Dame was playing Purdue. Rusty Lisch started the game but was having trouble with the Purdue defense. He was relieved by Gary Forystek in the second half. But when Forystek was sidelined by an injury, Lisch—not Montana—went into the game. Joe was miserable on the sidelines. He felt beaten. He says if he ever thought seriously about leaving football, it was at that moment.

Late in the third quarter, with Notre Dame down 24-14, Joe finally got into the game. He got off to a shaky start. He juggled his first snap from center and threw a wobbling, incomplete pass. But with the first nervousness gone, he drove Notre Dame to a field goal and two touchdowns. Notre Dame won, 31-24, and Joe had finally earned the starting quarterback spot. Notre Dame wouldn't lose for the rest of the season.

The Fighting Irish were invited to the Cotton Bowl to play against an undefeated University of Texas team that featured all-America running back Earl Campbell. Notre Dame outscored the Longhorns 14-0 in the second half and won 38-10. That season, Joe earned nicknames such as "Cool Joe" and "The Comeback Kid" as his reputation for clutch play grew.

Some thought Joe would be a candidate for the Heisman Trophy—the award made to the outstanding college football player—for the following year, 1978. But Notre Dame lost its first two games, and Joe threw two interceptions in each loss. His chance of winning the Heisman Trophy dimmed.

Joe had only three passes picked off for the rest of the season. Although he did not win the Heisman Trophy, he led the Irish to the 1979 Cotton Bowl against Houston. Joe says that Cotton Bowl game might be the most unusual game he has ever played. It is remembered as one of his greatest comeback victories.

Joe often felt defeated in college, but he hung on. He led Notre Dame to two Cotton Bowl victories and went on to a legendary pro career.

At game time the field was covered with ice. The temperature was 22° Fahrenheit (−5° Celsius) and the wind was whipping at 30 miles per hour (48 km/h)— somewhat unusual weather for Dallas, Texas. In an effort to melt the ice, the field crew threw rock salt on the field. But the salt only caused the players more pain when they were tackled. About 39,000 people who had tickets for the game decided to stay home.

Joe played poorly at first, mostly because he was freezing. By halftime his body temperature had dropped to 96° F (35° C) and he was shivering without control. During the half, attendants wrapped Joe in blankets and he drank as much hot chicken soup as he could.

Playing without Joe, Notre Dame found itself trailing, 34-12, late in the third quarter. That's when Joe came back in. Notre Dame rallied and, with two seconds left, Joe threw an 8-yard touchdown pass that tied the score, 34-34.

An extra point would win the game. Notre Dame's kick was good, but a penalty nullified the play. The second kick went through and Notre Dame captured a 35-34 victory in one of the wildest Cotton Bowl games in history.

The game was a fitting way for Joe to finish his college career. He had given Notre Dame one last comeback victory—the kind of victory that had built his reputation.

Joe graduated from Notre Dame in December 1978 with a business administration degree. He had concentrated his studies on marketing. Although Joe was certain to be a professional ball player, he had prepared himself well for another career. His confidence had grown since starting college and he found he liked being away from home. He moved to Los Angeles to make his home in a warm climate while he waited to be drafted into the National Football League in April. It was a welcome change from Pennsylvania and Indiana. Joe had "had enough of the windchill factor."

Joe was selected in the third round of the 1979 draft. He was the 82nd player picked and three quarterbacks were chosen before him. Some scouts called Joe inconsistent, jumpy, and not muscular enough to be a professional football player. Some said he wasn't strong enough to throw long passes and that he lacked control. Others believed Joe wasn't a hard worker in practice.

So despite his college reputation for coming through in the clutch, "The Comeback Kid" would have more proving to do in the pros. He would do it with the San Francisco 49ers, a team that had a record of 2-14 in the previous year.

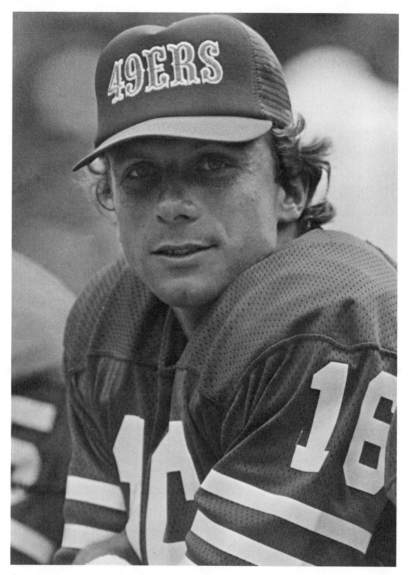

Joe became a 49er in 1979. Eleven years and four Super Bowls later, he had rewritten the record books.

3
Scrambling

During his first training camp with the San Francisco 49ers, Joe felt the pressure all rookies face. It was difficult to adjust to the pros' complicated system of plays. And Joe felt nervous until he knew for sure he had made the final roster cut and was on the team. Playing at Notre Dame wasn't like playing in the NFL, but at least it had introduced Joe to the pressure of national attention.

The 49ers had a new coach that 1979 season. His name was Bill Walsh and he had a reputation as a mastermind of offensive strategy. He had been an assistant coach in the NFL for 10 years and had helped develop several winning quarterbacks. Among his "students" were Ken Anderson, a top quarterback for the Cincinnati Bengals in the 1970s, and Dan Fouts, an outstanding passer for the San Diego Chargers during the same period.

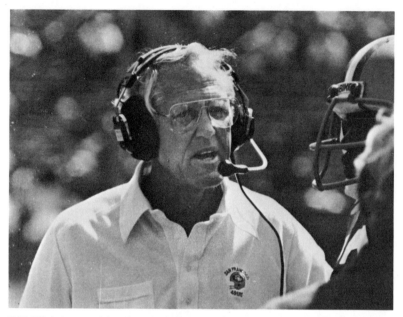

Bill Walsh would take the 49ers from a lackluster 2-14 record to a Super Bowl championship in just two seasons.

Walsh knew immediately that Joe was exceptionally quick on his feet and had an instinct for the parts of the game that can't be taught. But it commonly takes a pro quarterback a few years to develop into a regular— or starter—so for the present, Joe was expected to sit on the sidelines and learn. Joe was grateful that the great running back O.J. Simpson, who was in his final NFL season, took time to encourage him during this period.

On the field, the 49ers and starting quarterback Steve DeBerg were compiling another losing season.

Sometimes Joe felt it might be better that he *wasn't* getting to play. He could have been hurt physically by the superior opponents, or he might have begun to doubt his ability. Joe knew it was especially hard to play quarterback on a losing team. The opposition knows that a trailing team must pass to gain ground quickly, so they're well prepared to harass the passer.

Coach Walsh tried to break Joe in slowly. Sometimes he let Joe guide the team to a touchdown after a long drive by the 49ers. Joe also had the job of holding the ball for place kicks. Here Joe showed his steady hands and cool head. But he hated the job. Holding the football is a thankless duty. The holder often takes blame when a kick fails, but he almost never gets credit for the kicks that succeed.

The 49ers finished the 1979 season with a 2-14 record. It was no improvement over their 1978 mark. In the 1980 preseason, the team also played poorly. In Joe's first two starting assignments as a pro, the 49ers lost 21-0 and 48-0.

Montana and DeBerg were splitting the quarterback duties at this time and neither could win the job convincingly. Some rumors said the 49ers would trade for another quarterback because neither Montana nor DeBerg was getting the job done.

Joe and Steve were roommates, and they competed at everything from football to video baseball. When the regular season began, DeBerg had won the starting role. But the 49ers were still having problems. By the second half of the season, Walsh was leaning toward Joe as the number-one quarterback. Joe started the last four games of the season. In one game, the 49ers trailed New Orleans, 35-7, at halftime. But Joe rallied the 49ers to a 38-35 victory in overtime. The 28-point halftime deficit was the largest any team had overcome in NFL history.

Joe's comeback knack had not left him. He helped the 49ers finish with a 6-10 record that season. Just before the 1981 season, Steve DeBerg was traded to the Denver Broncos. Joe would be the 49ers' starting quarterback. Who knew how far he would take the team in the coming season?

Who would have thought that on January 10, 1982, the 49ers would be at Candlestick Park in San Francisco, playing the Dallas Cowboys for the National Football Conference title? It was more usual that the 49ers would be at home watching the conference championship game on television. Just two seasons before, the team had finished 2-14.

Even when the 1981 season began, the 49ers didn't look like division champions. They had a record of 1-2 after three games. They had impressed some people when they whipped the favored Cowboys, 45 to 14, in October. But even Bill Walsh said it would be a year or two before the 49ers could advance to the Super Bowl.

"It's not just the way he passes," says Joe's teammate Roger Craig, "it's his leadership in the huddle...he wants to win very badly."

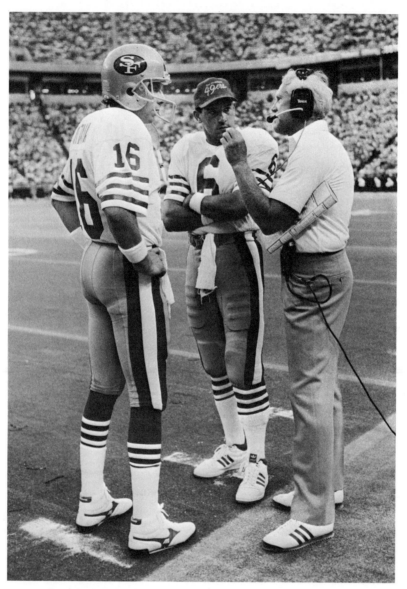

Coach Walsh plans strategy with his quarterbacks.

But the 49ers hung on to win the NFC Western Division title that season. They were the first NFL team to clinch a division title that year, and San Francisco's first NFL play-off team in nine years. In the NFC semifinal game, they defeated the New York Giants, 38-17. But the 49ers would have to face Dallas in the NFC championship game. The Cowboys had crushed Tampa Bay, 38-0, in the other NFC semifinal and they were eager to avenge their embarrassing loss to the 49ers from earlier in the year.

On game day, many of the 49ers were sick with the flu, but they played hard and kept the game close. Joe threw three interceptions, however, and the 49ers made six turnovers in all. Two turnovers led to touchdowns for the Cowboys. San Francisco also committed crucial penalties that led to 10 more points for Dallas.

With 4:54 left in the game, the 49ers trailed, 27-21. They had the ball on their own 11-yard line. It was too late for a field goal to help the 49ers. They had to have a touchdown. They needed Joe to get hot and take them all the way.

Some teams would have thrown long passes, hoping to gain the needed yards in a hurry. But the Dallas defense was set to stop such passes. So the 49ers decided to use short passes and running plays instead. This strategy asked a lot of the 49ers. They were an inexperienced team up against old pros. They would have to be cool and careful and hope their young quarterback could lead them.

The 49ers responded to the challenge. They zigzagged up the field in short- and medium-size bursts. Their wide-open passing game reminded some of the Cowboys of playground style football. But with 58 seconds left, the 49ers found themselves on the Cowboys' 6-yard line. It was third down and 3. San Francisco called a time-out.

It had been an exhausting drive. Wide receiver Dwight Clark sank to the ground asking for water. The Dallas defense looked weary and shocked at the same time. On the sidelines, Joe and Coach Walsh discussed what would be their biggest decision of the season.

The play they chose was a "sprint right option." Joe would try to hit wide receiver Freddie Solomon with a pass. But if Freddie were covered, Joe would try to find Dwight Clark. Joe promised to throw the ball out of bounds if the play wasn't "there."

When the ball was snapped, the Cowboys came charging. Running with the pack was 6-foot, 9-inch Ed "Too Tall" Jones. Joe saw that Solomon was covered, so he kept running to his right, looking for Clark. He would have to hurry. The Cowboys were coming fast.

Joe didn't actually see Clark break open. But after a season of practice, he knew where Clark would be.

Joe no longer throws his passes at a tire swing. Wide receiver Freddie Solomon has provided Joe with a faster moving target.

Wide receiver Dwight Clark grabbed the touchdown pass that gave the 49ers a 28-27 victory over Dallas and a ticket to the 1982 Super Bowl.

He pumped a fake with this throwing arm, then let the ball go high and hard over the rush into the end zone. He tried to throw it so that if Clark didn't get it, no one would.

Clark jumped high—higher than he thought he could—and came down with the ball. Joe couldn't see Dwight's catch. The Cowboys had flattened him. But Joe could hear the crowd and he knew the 49ers had scored.

With an extra point, San Francisco took a 28-27 lead. The Cowboys gave the 49ers a final scare with a rally on their last drive, but they couldn't score.

The 49ers were the NFC champs. They had gone 89 yards in 13 plays and won. The drama of the game's finish is still remembered by 49er fans as "The Drive" and "The Catch."

Joe passed out from exhaustion in the locker room after the game. He was too tired to celebrate. But he was ready two weeks later when the 49ers played the Cincinnati Bengals in Super Bowl XVI. The game would be played at the Silverdome in Pontiac, Michigan, where San Francisco had lost to the Detroit Lions in the first game of the season.

The 49ers had come a long way since then. But Joe admits he was nervous. He was worried about the Bengal defense and he was wary of making a big error. After all, this was his first Super Bowl.

The game began with the 49ers fumbling the opening kickoff. But Joe soon took control. He dived for a touchdown from the 1-yard line and threw an 11-yard touchdown pass to Earl Cooper. With two field goals from Ray Wersching, the 49ers took a 20-0 lead by halftime.

The Bengals rebounded in the second half, but a goal-line stand by the 49er defense in the third quarter helped break Cincinnati's momentum. The 49ers hung on and became Super Bowl champions with a 26-21 victory. Joe had completed 14 of 22 passes for 157 yards and was selected the game's Most Valuable Player.

But the 49ers' heroics in Super Bowl XVI could not help them in the 1982 season. They finished with a record of 3-6 in a season shortened by a players' strike.

The 49ers lost their first two games, and then the NFL players refused to compete for seven weeks. The players struck in protest against the team owners who, the players said, were treating them unfairly.

The strike lasted 57 days. Eight games were missed and only one was made up during the rest of the season. When the season resumed, the 49ers played well. But they did not win the division title that year, and they just missed earning a "wild card" spot that would have put them in the play-offs.

Statistically, it was a good year for Joe. But he played much of the year in pain. Long before the season began, he had minor surgery on his knee to remove torn cartilage. His throwing arm bothered him through the season and his ribs felt tender. He started wearing a "flak" jacket to protect his ribs.

In 1983, the 49ers needed to prove again that they were one of the league's top teams. They earned a 10-6 record and another chance at post-season play.

In the NFC divisional play-off, the 49ers won a nail-biting 24-23 victory over Detroit. The Lions missed a field goal with 10 seconds left in the game, and the 49ers advanced to face the Washington Redskins in the NFC title game.

After three quarters in the title game, the Redskins were leading, 21-0, and were humiliating the 49ers. But Joe threw three touchdown passes in the final period and the 49ers tied the score. Then with 40 seconds left in the game, Washington kicked a field goal and claimed a 24-21 victory.

Joe had passed for 347 yards in the game. But he was disgusted. The 49ers had come from so far behind only to lose to the Redskins. There was no way he could force himself to watch the Redskins play the Los Angeles Raiders in the Super Bowl. Instead, Joe vowed to bring the 49ers back.

4
Cool Joe

Joe Montana had more than football on his mind just before the 1984 season started. In August, Joe signed a six-year contract with the San Francisco 49ers for $6.6 million. At the time, it made Joe the highest-paid player in the NFL.

Also that month, Joe and his girlfriend Jennifer went for a walk in a park one day. Jennifer was an actress and a model, and Joe had met her while he was filming a television commercial. A lot of companies wanted famous athletes to promote their products and Joe Montana was in great demand for ads and commercials. His television appearances were no longer limited to football games. As Joe and Jennifer walked in the park that day, a plane flew overhead with a banner that said, "Jen Will You Marry Me? Joe." Jennifer knew who arranged the message, and she accepted.

Joe is a private person and he often finds it hard to be in the national spotlight. Joe is quiet until he gets to know someone. He seems calm and cool most of the time and some people have said he isn't very sensitive. This accusation bothers Joe. He says, "Sometimes I feel all the things people say I don't feel."

When he was a younger player, Joe became suspicious of people who wanted to be his friend just because he was a well-known athlete. Many people asked for Joe's time and he was afraid to tell them no. Now he is more careful about his schedule. Joe points out that college and pro athletes are very young when they start their careers. There is a lot of pressure on them to succeed. They are bound to make the mistakes any young person might make early in his or her career. Before he met Jennifer, Joe was married twice. He wasn't always happy in his personal life even though he was winning great acclaim as an athlete.

During hard times, Joe has always found refuge on the football field. He has never needed a coach's pep talk to get motivated for a game. The game itself has been his motivation.

On a typical day during the season, Joe's work begins at 8:30 A.M. He meets with other quarterbacks and some of the 49er coaches and watches films of upcoming opponents. Practice begins after lunch. The 49ers work out for about two hours in the afternoon and then the team gathers for another meeting.

Joe starts work at 8:30 A.M. He practices, watches game films, and meets with the team and coaches. Even at home, Joe has to spend several hours studying new plays for the next game.

At home, after dinner, Joe spends about two more hours studying new plays. He usually only goes out on Sunday night after a game, or on Monday—the night before his day off. Joe frankly calls practice "drudgery" and he is glad when game day rolls around.

As Joe and Jennifer were making plans for the future in the fall of 1984, the 49ers were getting off to a fast start. Early in the year, they posted a 37-31 victory over the Washington Redskins before a Monday night television audience. It was sweet revenge for Joe and the 49ers to defeat the defending Super Bowl champions.

San Francisco then knocked off the New Orleans Saints, but Joe bruised his ribs in the game. He missed his first start in 49 games the next week. But Joe returned in the following game and led San Francisco past the New York Giants, 31-10.

The 49ers rolled over most of their competition in 1984, winning many games by large margins. They had 15 victories in one season—more than any team in NFL history.

As division champions, the 49ers met the New York Giants in the first round of post-season play. San Francisco won, 21-10, and then became the NFC champion by quieting the Chicago Bears, 23-0. It was a good game to win handily, because some of the Bears had been boastful before the game.

San Francisco came into Super Bowl XIX as the

three-point favorite over the Miami Dolphins. Yet despite the 49ers' dominant year, much of the talk before the game was about the Dolphins and their flashy young quarterback, Dan Marino.

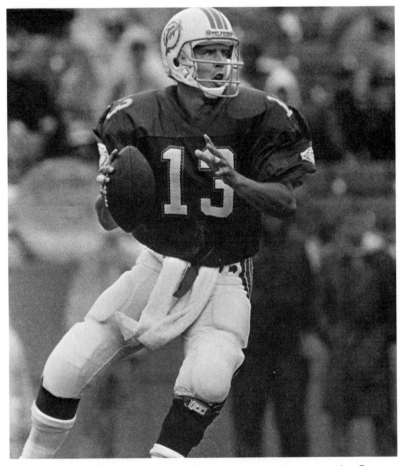

Miami's Dan Marino. Would he upstage Montana in Super Bowl XIX?

In his second year, Marino had led Miami to a 16-2 record. He had set a season record that year by throwing 48 touchdown passes. At 23 he was the youngest quarterback to start in a Super Bowl. The 84,059 fans who came to Stanford Stadium in Palo Alto, California, expected to see a dramatic showdown between two talented teams and their quarterbacks. Joe wanted to be sure he came out on top. Once again he was ready for the big game.

Marino played well, but he couldn't handle the 49ers. San Francisco came away with a 38-16 victory. The 49er defense had sacked Marino four times and intercepted two of his passes. Marino completed 29 of 50 passes for 318 yards. But Joe connected on 24 of 35 attempts for 331 yards and three touchdowns. It was a performance that earned him the Most Valuable Player Award in the Super Bowl for the second time.

Joe was proud. Once again he had come through in a big game. He and the 49ers had erased the memory of being eliminated by the Redskins the year before. He was the NFC's top-rated passer and was selected to the Pro Bowl team. Yet there was more to accomplish, and obstacles ahead.

5

Quarterback Sack

Joe Montana's back was hurting when he reported to training camp for the 1985 season. He twisted it further in a pre-season game against the Denver Broncos and the pain was so bad he couldn't practice the following week.

Joe had been born with scoliosis, an irregular curvature of the spine. This was part of the problem. The other part was the pounding he took being a quarterback in the NFL.

Joe missed the last two pre-season games and, when the season began, he still felt pain. But he played in spite of it. He exercised his back by walking in a swimming pool and he received medical treatment through the season. He also learned to bend and fall in ways that would put the least strain on his back.

In the season's first game, the 49ers made seven turnovers and lost to the Minnesota Vikings, 28-21.

Joe is on the run, looking for an open receiver. He only has a few seconds to react before the defense closes in on him.

San Francisco won five of its next six games, but sometimes winning was difficult.

Despite his health problems, Joe had a fine year. He led the NFC with 303 completions and 3,653 yards passing. He compiled two streaks of more than 100 passes without an interception. He also was selected to the Pro Bowl, athough yet another health problem—a shoulder injury—kept him out of the game.

Yet some critics thought Joe's performance was sagging. They spread rumors that Joe was abusing drugs. The rumors hurt Joe. He had trouble sleeping and he wondered if playing football was worth facing public suspicion. Because several well-known athletes had been found to use drugs, Joe knew that people now wondered about drug use among all athletes— especially famous quarterbacks. Joe eventually appeared at a press conference to deny the accusations and clear the air about drugs.

The 49ers lost the 1985 NFC Western Division title to the Los Angeles Rams, but they gained a play-off berth as a "wild card" team. In the play-off game, the New York Giants shut Joe and the 49ers out of the end zone, handing them a 17-3 defeat.

Although the 1985 season was difficult, the 1986 season presented Joe with one of the greatest challenges he had ever faced. In the season opener against Tampa Bay, Joe again twisted his back. It happened in the third quarter while he was rolling out, trying to pass to Dwight Clark. Joe stayed in the game and wound up with 356 yards passing in the 31-7 victory. But the next day, Joe's back hurt so much that he couldn't stand or lift his legs.

X-rays showed that the lowest movable disk in Joe's spine had ruptured. Disks are like shock absorbers between the bones of the spine, and when a disk is damaged, the back loses some of its cushioning. On September 15, Joe underwent surgery. In a two-hour operation, doctors removed a third of the damaged disk. The doctors called the surgery a success, but they were not sure Joe could ever play football again. Surely, he would miss the rest of the season.

Joe was depressed after hearing the news. But comebacks are his specialty, and Joe was determined to play again. He was jogging and doing light exercise within two weeks of the surgery, and he was throwing a football within a month.

Soon Joe was pushing himself three hours a day— running, swimming, and lifting weights. By November 9, less than two months after his injury, Joe was ready to play against the St. Louis Cardinals in Candlestick Park. He was expected to wear a back brace in the game, but he chose not to because the brace made it hard for him to breathe. Instead, Joe left the Cardinals gasping by throwing touchdown passes of 45, 40, and 44 yards in a 43-17 victory.

Doctors said Joe might never play football again. But, less than two months after undergoing surgery on his lower back, Joe was winning football games.

The 49ers won five of their last seven games after Joe's return and earned a spot in the play-offs. But the New York Giants eliminated the 49ers in the first game of the postseason with a 49-3 victory. Late in the second quarter, Joe suffered a concussion and left the game. It was a painful end to a painful season.

But it also was a season of triumph. Joe had completed 191 of 307 passes for 2,236 yards and eight touchdowns. Not bad for a man who was supposed to be out for the year.

The following season, 1987, was full of more surprises. The 49ers stumbled in a 30-17 loss to Pittsburgh in the season opener. Joe threw three interceptions. But the next week against Cincinnati, Joe and the team were back to their comeback best. With two seconds left in the game, Joe threw a 25-yard touchdown pass to Jerry Rice and San Francisco came away with a 27-20 victory.

The following week, the NFL players went on strike again. All games were cancelled. Again, the players refused to play in protest against the policies of the team owners. This time the owners countered by hiring a whole new set of athletes to wear the official NFL uniforms. The replacements began play in the fourth week of the season.

Some NFL players did not go along with the strike and chose to play alongside the replacement players. Although Joe sat out from the first "replacement" game, he played the following two games. After 24 days, the strike was over and the regular players returned.

The NFL ruled that the games played by the stand-ins would count in the final standings. The 49ers were fortunate that their replacements had won all three games during the strike. When the regular 49ers returned, they won 9 of their last 10 games and posted the best record in the NFL.

In the third-to-last game of the season, Joe strained muscles in the back of his left thigh. The injury put him on the bench during the 49ers' 41-0 victory over the Chicago Bears. He was replaced by Steve Young, a former college star at Brigham Young University.

Joe didn't start a game again until the 49ers met the Minnesota Vikings in the NFC divisional play-off game. For the first time all season, the 49ers didn't score a touchdown in the first half. Joe was sacked four times and threw an interception that was returned 45 yards for a touchdown. Midway through the third quarter, Joe was replaced by Steve Young. It was the first time since Joe had become a starter that he was pulled from a game in favor of another quarterback.

Young quickly took the 49ers in to score, but the Vikings went on to win 36-24. For the third straight year, San Francisco had been eliminated in the first game of the play-offs.

Despite the sour ending, it was another good year

for Joe. If his health remained stable, Joe could lead the 49ers to another big year. Yet he would have to meet the quarterback challenge of his teammate Steve Young.

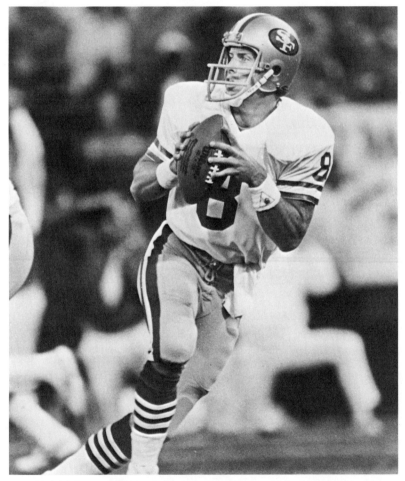

Would Steve Young take the starting spot from Montana?

6

State of Montana

Joe Montana might be traded, went the rumors in the off-season. Some people said that, at age 32, Montana's great days were over. Coach Bill Walsh did not make it clear who would be the 49ers' starting quarterback in the coming season. He left the question hanging until late in training camp.

Walsh was impressed with Steve Young, who was 27 and a gifted athlete. Some thought Walsh wanted to groom Young for the starting job and phase out Montana.

Walsh told the media that Joe would be the starting quarterback "as long as he's healthy." But that statement didn't settle the issue. Joe had a history of back, rib, and arm problems, and he might never be in perfect shape. Still, Joe felt well enough to give his best, and he didn't want the question of his health to be an excuse to let Steve Young play instead of him.

Joe started the season opener against New Orleans and the 49ers won with a late field goal. But Joe did not play the fourth quarter because of a bruised elbow. Young started the next week against the New York Giants, but Joe came in at the start of the second half. With 42 seconds left in the game, Joe threw a 78-yard touchdown pass to Jerry Rice and the 49ers won, 20-17.

Still, Joe played an entire game only twice in the first half of the season. Both his bruised ribs and his sore elbow hurt him. He played erratically, sometimes throwing bad passes that were intercepted. For the first time since the 1981 season, Joe went three games at one stretch without throwing a touchdown pass. Coach Walsh replaced Joe with Steve Young in the middle of some games, hoping to improve the 49ers' offense.

Joe admitted he felt tentative on the field, knowing in the back of his mind that he might be pulled out of the game. "I never doubted myself," Joe said, "but sometimes you wonder a little. I just had to remain positive."

Young was the starting quarterback in a 24-21 victory over the Minnesota Vikings and was voted NFC Offensive Player of the Week. But he often played poorly, and so did the team. After a 9-3 loss to the Los Angeles Raiders, the 49ers were 6 and 5 and in third place in their division.

Although Joe and Coach Walsh would disagree many times through the years, the two would combine to make San Francisco one of the most powerful offensive teams of the 1980s.

The play-offs and Super Bowl seemed remote, and there was speculation that Coach Walsh's job was in trouble. But the 49ers were known to play well late in the season. They won four of their last five games and made the play-offs for the sixth straight year. From 1983 through 1988, the 49ers' record in the last four games of season was 17-3—best in the NFL.

The 49ers faced Minnesota in the NFC divisional play-off. The Vikings sported the league's top defense, and Joe dodged a stiff pass rush all day. But the 49ers' offensive line held, and Joe was sacked only one time. Joe threw three touchdown passes to Jerry Rice in the first half and the 49ers won, 34-9.

The NFC championship game against the Bears was played January 8, 1989, in Chicago's Soldier Field. The temperature was 17° F (−8° C) with a windchill factor of −26° F (−32° C). The ground froze and became more slick as the game went on. Many players changed from cleats to rubber-soled shoes.

The cold weather made it difficult for Joe to throw accurate passes. It's hard to grip the ball with frozen fingers. Joe wore a glove on his left hand and kept hand warmers in the pockets of his jersey. The warmers generate heat by a chemical process. They cooled quickly in the freezing weather, and Joe would get new warmers each time he took the field.

The warmers must have helped, because Joe was hot. He connected on 17 of 27 passes for 288 yards and three touchdowns, and led the 49ers to a 28-3 victory. The 49ers were super again, and they proved it further against the Cincinnati Bengals in the Super Bowl two weeks later in Miami. That was the day Joe and the 49ers rallied to their third Super Bowl victory with a last-minute touchdown drive.

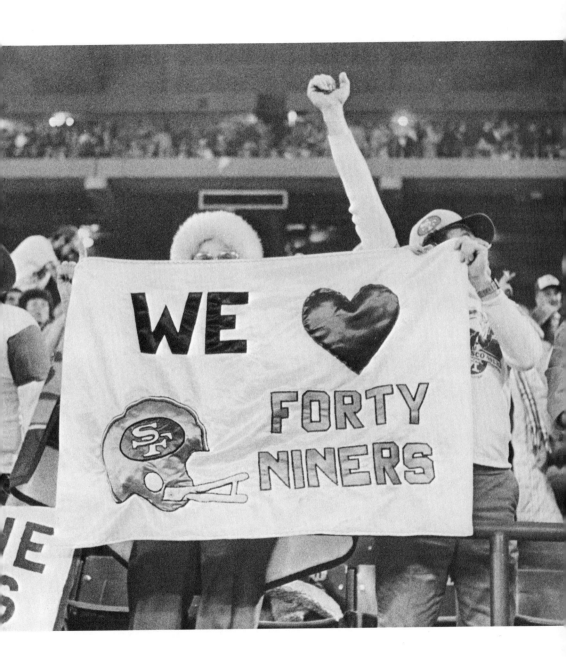

"I think it's probably the best drive ever," Joe said, reflecting on the clutch comebacks of his career. "It's got to rank up there, believe me. The one thing we never gave up on was confidence."

Joe Montana had delivered again. When the season began he couldn't claim to be the starting quarterback, but now his peers were comparing him with the best ever to play the game.

Joe and Freddie Solomon chat on the sidelines.

The 1989 season presented San Francisco with a fresh test. Bill Walsh stepped down and was replaced by assistant coach George Seifert. Many people wondered if Joe would be as dangerous playing for a new head coach. Others thought that Joe's repeated injuries would slow him down. Could San Francisco produce another championship season?

Joe and the 49ers responded to the critics with a remarkable year. Joe completed more than 70 percent of his passes and threw 26 touchdown passes. The 49ers romped to a 14-2 record during the regular season, breezed through the playoffs, and found themselves preparing for their fourth Super Bowl.

They were heavy favorites and they crushed the Denver Broncos, 55-10. Joe threw five touchdown passes and finished the game with eight Super Bowl records. He was named Super Bowl MVP for the third time. Now experts were calling him the finest quarterback of all time.

"I don't think you can go wrong saying Montana is the best quarterback in history," said Joe Namath, former star quarterback for the New York Jets.

Joe and the 49ers looked unstoppable in 1990. Joe's precision passing brought San Francisco to the top of the NFL with a 15-2 record in the regular season. *Sports Illustrated* magazine named Joe its Sportsman of the Year.

The 49ers were favored to beat the New York Giants

in the NFC conference championship game and were expected to continue on to their third Super Bowl in three years. But Joe's game was off, and New York held San Francisco to just 13 points. With only 4 seconds left on the clock, the Giants kicked a field goal and squeezed by with a 15-13 victory.

Joe was hit hard late in the game, and X rays revealed a broken bone in his right hand. Instead of another trip to the Super Bowl, a disappointed 49er team headed home.

Joe and Jennifer have three children, Alexandra, Elizabeth, and Nathaniel. The Montanas have settled in Redwood City, California. But for now, Joe's other home is the football field. "If we keep playing like this, I can play until I'm 40," Joe says. The "Comeback Quarterback" plans to keep coming back.

JOE MONTANA
San Francisco 49ers
NFL statistics

Passing

YEAR	GAMES	ATTEMPTS	COMPLETIONS	PERCENTAGE	GAIN	TOUCHDOWN PASSES	PASS INTERCEPTIONS
1979	16	23	13	56.5	96	1	0
1980	15	273	176	64.5	1795	15	9
1981	16	488	311	63.7	3565	19	12
1982	9	346	213	61.6	2613	17	11
1983	16	515	332	64.5	3910	26	12
1984	16	432	279	64.6	3630	28	10
1985	15	494	303	61.3	3653	27	13
1986	8	307	191	62.2	2236	8	9
1987	13	398	266	66.8	3054	31	13
1988	14	397	238	59.9	2981	18	10
1989	13	386	271	70.2	3521	26	8
1990	15	520	321	61.7	3944	26	16

Rushing

YEAR	ATTEMPTS	YARDS	AVERAGE	TOUCHDOWNS
1979	3	22	7.3	0
1980	32	77	2.4	2
1981	25	95	3.8	2
1982	30	118	3.9	1
1983	61	284	4.7	2
1984	39	118	3.0	2
1985	42	153	3.6	3
1986	17	38	2.2	0
1987	35	141	4.0	1
1988	38	132	3.5	3
1989	49	227	4.6	3
1990	40	162	4.1	1

ACKNOWLEDGMENTS

Photographs are reproduced through the courtesy of: Vernon J. Biever, pp. 1, 2, 6, 8, 31, 48, 59; San Francisco 49ers, pp. 11, 26, 28, 35, 36, 51, 54; Michael Zagaris, pp. 14, 23, 32, 39, 40, 43, 57, 60, 64; New York Jets Football Club, p. 16; University of Notre Dame, p. 20; Miami Dolphins, p. 45. Front and back cover: Michael Zagaris.